The Beauty of Ramadan

꙳ ꙳ ꙳ ꙳ ꙳

A Guide to the Muslim Month

of Prayer and Fasting

In the Name of God

Most Gracious, Ever So Merciful,

With Daily and Humble Thanks.

With Contributions From

Imam Sayed Hassan Qazwini

Hiba Hassan

David Crumm

Eide Alawan

John Hile

And Support From

Allie, Nadia, Tarik, Bilal And Yusef

Third Edition
Published by:
Read The Spirit Books
an imprint of
David Crumm Media, LLC
Canton, Michigan

For those who believe and work righteousness there is every blessing and a beautiful place of return for eternity.

— Quran, Chapter 13, The Thunder, Al Raad, Verse 29

The breath of a fasting person is the most fragrant scent to God.

— Prophet Muhammad (pbuh)

Contents

Author's Note

This booklet is as a simplified guide to Muslim practices during the holy month of Ramadan. I have prepared the book for Muslims and non-Muslims alike, hoping that non-Muslims will find this a helpful window into our religious traditions – and Muslims will use this as a refresher in recalling the richness of our faith.

Non-Muslim readers will find not only the heart of Ramadan in this book, but also many of our specific religious customs, such as adding "(pbuh)" after mentioning the name the prophetic founder of Islam. We try to be as respectful as possible in approaching our faith and the (pbuh) notation is our reminder that, when we recall his name, we always add: "peace be upon him." We also do this with other great prophets including Abraham (pbuh), Moses (pbuh) and Jesus (pubh). So, as you read this guide, you'll find not only the core story of Ramadan, but you'll also see how we approach and live out our religious traditions day by day.

That approach also makes this handbook useful for teachers, students, interfaith leaders, health-care workers and other professionals who wish to encourage and discuss the similarities between various cultures and faiths. You can join in the ongoing dialogue by visiting www.SharingRamadan.info

In Peace,
Najah Bazzy, R.N.
Transcultural Nurse Specialist

Preparing Our Hearts and Minds

The Blessing of the Holy Month of Ramadan

In this holy and sacred month, the doors of Heaven are open. A person who understands the glory of this month will take advantage of the Divine Mercy that is offered by God. Let us take time to find a quiet and private place – lower our heads in humility and raise our hearts in praise.

God says that humanity is His crowning creation for we have the gift of the intellect and intelligence. God has granted humanity this intellect with a free will to choose God or not. If we wish to communicate our deepest needs, cleanse our conscience, or ask for forgiveness, then we should know that Ramadan is the best of months. Consider where you are in your spiritual life and measure that journey by how you feel when the Month of Ramadan ends.

We can all choose to develop the spiritual awareness and enlightenment by tuning in to listen quietly to the voice of our soul. When our soul or inner being whispers we must try to block the outside signals that clog and clutter the spiritual inner voice. We must train ourselves so we can hear what that voice is saying loud and clear, rather than the muffled version the majority of us live with.

Find an inspirational story or figure. There are many books about the Prophet Muhammad (pbuh) and his progeny that can serve as inspiration, not to mention the beautiful Holy Quran, which embrace the words and advice of God Almighty. The language of the Holy Quran renews itself every time you read it. Let us use the legacy of the Messengers of God to help create our own life force. Let us ask God in all His majesty to purify the heart, expand the mind, and enlighten the spirit with piety and humility.

Islam focuses on promoting the unity of the mind, body, and soul so that spiritual balance exists. During this month, the reward for giving charity to the poor and orphaned is among the best of deeds, and our deeds are multiplied during this blessed month. Give generously to charity so that in return we receive God's mercy, forgiveness, and eternal reward.

> Feeding a person when it is time to break the fast is the equivalent of freeing a person held in bondage. Your past sins are forgiven even if all that you offer is a portion of a date or a drink of water for this will give you immunity and protection for eternity.
>
> — *Prophet Muhammad (pbuh)*

Prophet Muhammad (pbuh) warns that your soul is linked to your deeds and your deeds are linked to your will, and this month your will is free from the evils of (Satan) so all advantages belong to you and are for you. Keep the best of relations with your family and relatives, and be kind to the elderly. Love yourself enough to reserve your place in heaven by calling upon your Creator to strengthen you with knowledge and wisdom. God has instructed Prophet Muhammad (pbuh) to teach humankind this direct Divine wisdom known as Hadith Qudsi.

All the deeds of humankind are for you except for the deed of fasting, which belongs to Me, and it is I who reward him/her for this deed

— *God.*

Sermon on the Reception of the Holy Month of Ramadan

This famous sermon by the Prophet Muhammad (pbuh) describes the way Muslims should welcome the month of Ramadan:

O People! The month of God (Ramadhan) has approached you with His mercy and blessings. This is the month that is the best of all months in the estimation of God. Its days are the best among the days; its nights are the best among the nights. Its hours are the best among the hours.

This is a month in which He has invited you. You have been, in this month, selected as the recipients of the honors of God, the Merciful. In this holy month, when you breathe, it has the heavenly reward of the praise of God on rosary beads (tasbeeh), and your sleep has the reward of worship.

Your good deeds are accepted in this month. So are your invocations. Therefore, you must invoke your Lord, in right earnest, with hearts that are free from sins and evils, that God may bless you. Observe fast, in this month, and recite the Holy Quran.

Verily! The person who may not receive the mercy and benevolence of God in this month must be very unfortunate having an end as bad (in the Hereafter). While fasting, remember the hunger and thirst of tomorrow in eternity.

Give alms to the poor and the needy. Pay respect to your elders.

Have pity on those younger than you and be kind towards your relatives and kinsmen. Guard your tongues against unworthy words, and your eyes from such scenes that are not worth seeing (forbidden) and your ears from such sounds that should not be heard by you.

Be kind to orphans so that if your children become orphans they also may be treated with kindness. Do invoke God that He may forgive your sins. Do raise your hands at the time of Salat (Prayers), as it is the best time for asking His mercy. When we invoke at such times, we are answered by Him, when we call Him, He responds, and when we ask for anything, it is accepted by Him.

O People! You have made your conscience the slave of your desires; make it free by invoking Him for repentance and forgiveness. Your back is breaking under the heavy load of your sins, so prostrate before Him for long intervals and lighten your load.

Do understand fully well that God has promised in the name of His Majesty and Honor that He will not take to task such people who fast and offer prayers in this month and perform prostration, and will guard their bodies against the punishment on the Day of Judgment.

O People! If anybody amongst you arranges for the Iftar (food for the ending of the fast) of any believer, then God will give you a reward as if you have set free a slave. He will forgive your minor sins.

Then the companions of Holy Prophet Muhammad (pbuh) said: "But everybody amongst us does not have the means to do so?"

Holy Prophet Muhammad (pbuh) told them: Keep yourself away from God's wrath, by inviting for Iftar, though it may consist of only half a date or simply with water if you have nothing else. O People! Anybody who may cultivate good manners in this month will walk over the bridge to the next life with ease, though his feet may be shaking.

Anybody who in this month may take light work from his servants (male or female), God will make easy his accounting on the Day of Judgment.

Anybody who covers the faults of others in this month, God will cover his faults in this life and in eternity. Anybody, who respects and treats an orphan with kindness in this month, God shall look at him with dignity in the Hereafter. Anybody who treats well his kinsmen, in this month, God will bestow His mercy on him, while anybody who mistreats his kinsmen in this month, God will keep him away from His mercy.

Whoever offers a recommended prayer in this month, God will give him freedom from Hell. Whosoever offers one obligatory prayer in this month, for him the Angels will write the rewards of 70 such prayers, which were offered by him in any other month.

Whosoever recites repeatedly Peace and blessings upon me, God will keep the scales of his good deeds heavy, (promising heaven) when in the Hereafter the scales of others will be light. (which earns God's disappointment)

Islamic Perspectives on Fasting

What does the word "Ramadan" mean?

Do not say the word Ramadan for it is a name belonging
to God but rather say the Month of Ramadan.

— *Prophet Muhammad (pbuh)*

Ramadan is one of the beautiful names of God and the word itself
is an attribute that glorifies God. The word has several historic
references. The first is that the word Ramadan was revealed to the Holy
Prophet Muhammad (pbuh) almost 15 years after he began to receive
his divine call or revelation while he lived in his host and holy city of
Medina, in Arabia, which is now known as Saudi Arabia.

The second historic reference deals with the literal translation of the
word Ramadan, which has its root in the Arabic language and trans-
lates most closely to the meaning "to extinguish." In this context, it

would mean that God is the *Extinguisher of Sins* and that with God alone is the ability to forgive a believing servant. Hence, the month of Ramadan is a Holy Name and can be considered an attribute of God. It is always best to preface the word by saying, "the Month of Ramadan" rather than to say Ramadan. Out of respect for God, this would be the observant and humble manner of one who is pious before the Magnificent Creator.

The word Ramadan also represents the name of the ninth lunar month as set forth in the Islamic calendar. Each year the fast occurs in this ninth lunar month. The significance of the month is overwhelming for any devout Muslim and adhering to the fast is a discipline that represents inner strength, devotion, and commitment to what is believed to be a divine command. Muslims believe this command was decreed directly by God to humankind.

Throughout religious history, there have been many quotes by prophets and saints that glorify the bounty of fasting from different faith traditions. There is much wisdom that can be gleaned from these traditions for the personal and collective good of humanity. Fasting teaches us lessons from humility to economic equity.

Let us examine this quote from Imam Ja'far as-Sadiq, who was a scholarly Imam. He is also the founder of the first "university of jurisprudence" in Islam. He would be the sixth revered Saint that comes from the Prophet Muhammad's (pbuh) lineage according to Shia Muslims, and a prominent thinker and highly respected leader of jurist law according to all Muslims.

> The wisdom behind fasting is to equalize between rich and poor thus if it were not for fasting the wealthy would never feel the pains of hunger; God wanted to bring balance amongst His servants by making those with bounty feel the conditions of the less fortunate.
>
> — *Imam Ja' far as-Sadiq*

When does the month of Ramadan begin and end?

The fast follows the lunar calendar, so it begins and ends with the sighting of the moon. The moon has served humankind since creation by setting the calendar for fixed seasons long before the advancement of time-telling devices. The moon is reliable, authentic, and universal and is a symbol to be shared by people throughout the world. A lunar month can never be less than 29 days or more than 30 days.

According to Islamic jurisprudence, the moon must be seen by two people who are "just and trustworthy." Their testimony would suffice to begin the month of fast. These days it is customary to entrust your fast to your local Masjid (mosque) or religious leader to help guide you or the congregation. It is possible but difficult for the moon to be sighted on the actual day that it is born due to its orbit. If it were visible to the naked eye, it would be for a very short time only at the time of dusk until nightfall under the clearest skies. Often people would fast the day of the new moon as a precaution though it may not be visible and call this a "day of doubt." If the new moon were sighted the following day then that would mark the first day of Ramadan.

The first day of Ramadan moves back approximately ten to eleven days every year in the Gregorian solar calendar. It should also be noted that with the advancement of science, many Muslims depend on scientific findings such as that of NASA to determine the birth of the new moon.

Why Should a Person Fast?

We should turn, first, to the Quran to explore and understand the significance of the fast. The Holy Quran is a dialogue between God and humankind according to Islamic belief and practices. God commands us to read and contemplate the reality of His divine message through this Holy Scripture. When we read the Holy Quran, the

Almighty Magnificent God is speaking to each of us as His individual creation.

God offers us guidance that is specific to our healthy and holy living. God makes clear His mercy upon each person when He addresses the concept of the fast. This particular Quranic verse demonstrates that fasting is not a new idea given to Muslims, but was given as divine decree to both Jews and Christians as well.

> O you who believe! Fasting is prescribed (or ordained) for you, even as it was prescribed to those before you, that ye might learn self – restraint.
>
> — *Quran, Chapter 2, The Cow, Al Baqarah, Verse 183*

Let us examine this verse in its simplest application. When one goes to the physician due to illness or a disease of the body or mind, the doctor prescribes a treatment to help one feel better and gain quality of health. The physician is compensated to do this – but God receives nothing in return nor requires any compensation to prescribe a holistic treatment such as fasting, which promotes optimum balance of the mind, body, and spirit. In addition, there is great reward beyond human comprehension for the person who participates in God's prescribed way of living. This reward or benefit is not only for the here and for now. God promises that the fast will continue to demonstrate its merit in a person's eternal life by giving the fasting person all that they desire in heaven.

For a devout and practicing Muslim this act of fasting is tied to the profound Mercy of God. Fasting allows for a connection to the Divine Essence, which fills the heart with a renewed spirit. Prophet Muhammad (pbuh) teaches Muslims the following, words often repeated during the holy month.

> If a servant of God understands the mercy of the Holy Month of Ramadan then they would wish for Ramadan to be the whole year.
>
> — *Prophet Muhammad (pbuh)*

For the fasting person there are two joys. One when they break their fast and the other when they meet their Lord.

— *Prophet Muhammad (pbuh)*

God continues this merciful dialogue with humankind in the Holy Quran. God makes clear the rationale for the prescribed fast:

Ramadan is the month in which was sent down the Quran as a guide to humankind also clear (Signs) for guidance and judgment (between right and wrong). So every one of you who is present (at his home) during that month should spend it in fasting but if anyone of you is ill or on a journey the prescribed period (should be made up) by days later. God intends every facility for you. He does not want to put you through difficulty. He wants you to complete the prescribed period and to glorify Him in that He has guided you: and perchance ye shall be grateful.

— *Quran, Chapter 2, Al Baqarah, The Cow, Verse 185*

Why We Fast

The Prophet Muhammad (pbuh) was a guide for humankind. While the Holy Quran is the oral communication between the Creator and the created, the Prophet Muhammad (pbuh) is said to be the living Quran. For Muslims, the Prophet Muhammad (pbuh) embodied the values of the Holy Scripture. He imparted the following wisdom to Muslims during the Month of Ramadan. Here we learn that fasting is tied to a very different kind of charity.

> Everything has a charity and the charity of your body is your fast. ...
>
> Fast to be healthy.
>
> — *Prophet Muhammad (pbuh)*

Healthy and Helpful in Many Ways

There are many benefits for the fasting person, including the physical, psychological, spiritual, and social domain. Islam is very careful to encourage Muslims to be moderate in all things, to strive to find the correct balance in life. The human body is an incredible instrument and therefore Islam believes in keeping this carrying case for the soul as pure as can be. A key concept in Islam is to cleanse oneself from physical impurities before prayer through a ritual wash. The logical mind can also deduce that the cleansing of the inner body is as important as the outer body. The fast in many ways can be thought of as the "inner cleanse."

These days the West is borrowing many of the Eastern ideas of health such as bowel cleansing with health experts commenting daily on the benefits of such practices. When a person fasts, the gastrointestinal tract is allowed to rest, which is important especially in a society that suffers from obesity. Cholesterol levels may be lowered as a result of a decrease in fatty snacks, hydrogenated oils, fast food, and high fructose syrups that drench our daily diets. Our bodies rest from caffeine and refined sugar intake. Our lungs and respiratory tract are able to recuperate from the heavy intake of cigarette smoke and addictive nicotine since smoking is also prohibited during the fasting hours. The physical body needs a time out and that is exactly what the All-Knowing Creator ordered.

A person finds that fasting exercises the brain and decreases the cravings we have for sugar and habitual snacking after the first three days. The brain is a selfish organ interested in self-satisfaction and self-survival. Fasting exercises our willpower to boost our brainpower by utilizing the concept of mind over matter. God clearly recognizes this effort and challenge to refrain from food and drink and compensates the fasting person. Prophet Muhammad (pbuh) teaches us God's mercy in this next wisdom as we see how God obligates Himself to each observant faster.

> For the person who is barred from food he loves due to his observance of fast, it will be mandatory upon God to provide him from the food and drink of heaven.
>
> — *Prophet Muhammad (pbuh)*

Psychological Benefits

Exercising a person's will power to refrain from the everyday dependency on food, drink, smoke, sex and other basic human needs teaches our very selfish brain to be that which it is not – disciplined! Having the ability to say "NO" teaches the lesson of self-control. Self-control is paramount in having a morally mindful and God-conscious personality. Health-care providers have been using behavior modification techniques quite a bit in recent years, especially for weight control, drug abuse, and other physical, mental, or emotional disorders. However, God has ordained fast as a behavior modification for thousands of years in our human history.

Fasting is more than refraining from food and drink. It is also a moral commitment to enjoin good and forbid that which is bad at the personal, family and community level. These principles encourage a sense of inner growth and development as you feel the cultivation of your spirit expand. This small story gives us a glimpse of how important the spirituality of the fast is to our well-being.

> Prophet Muhammad (pbuh) heard a woman swearing and cursing her servant. He called upon someone to bring food and said to her, "Eat."
>
> Quite shocked by the Prophet Muhammad's (pbuh) request, she replied, "I cannot eat for I am fasting O Messenger of God."
>
> The Prophet Muhammad (pbuh) replied, "How can you be fasting when you just cursed your servant? Fasting is not only from food and drink but God also ordains that fasting is to guard yourself against sins whether in your actions or in your words."

The Prophet Muhammad (pbuh) then continued imparting wisdom by saying this:

"How few are those who truly fast and how many are those who know only hunger.

There could be those that would gain nothing from the rewards of their fast except for hunger and thirst."

Spiritual Benefits

The spiritual benefit is profoundly different for each person. This depends on your spiritual ladder toward self-development. It is in this month that each person regardless of their station in life, gender, age, knowledge, accomplishments, wealth, or poverty should focus on exercising their spiritual self through repentance, self-reflection, and dialogue with God. No matter what condition a person is experiencing in life during the Holy Month of Ramadan there exits an open door called supplication or the act of invoking God's mercy.

This means that a person takes the time to sit quietly and dialogue with the Divine. Alternatively, for the better-developed Muslim spirit, this is a constant state of the heart. It becomes an almost unconscious language that goes on all day as the soul whispers lovingly and converses with the Creator. It is highly advised by God to take advantage of the divine mercy and love that is so abundantly raining down from the heavens during this holy time. The Holy Month of Ramadan is truly the new year from which resolutions should be born and the human spirit strengthened.

This is the time for spiritual alignment for anyone seeking a new direction or the sublime dimension of "self building," a spiritual phrase commonly used in Islam. During the fast one is working on their daily struggle to submit to this Divine alignment through one's own free will and intellect. Hence the true definition of Islam is the peace-fulfilling submission to the worship and will of God in His Infinite Glory and Manifestation.

Consider the following wisdom:

> Your sleeping is worship, even your silence is glory, and
> your supplications are heard and your deeds are multiplied,
> and at the moment of your breaking of fast, your requests
> and prayers are heard.
>
> — *Prophet Muhammad (pbuh)*

> The fasting spirit of the heart is greater than the fasting of
> the tongue, and the fasting of the tongue is greater than
> the fasting of the stomach.
>
> — *Prophet Muhammad (pbuh)*

> Prophet Muhammad (pbuh) said to his companion Jabir,
> "Oh, Jabir this is the Month of Ramadan. Whomever shall
> fast the daytime of Ramadan and spend the night time in
> prayer, and guard their stomach and physical urges (sexual
> desire and genitalia) from that which is forbidden (during
> the fasting hours) and protects their tongue (from gos-
> sip) – leaves behind their sins as someone leaves behind the
> passing Month of Ramadan."
>
> And so replied Jabir, "What a beautiful wisdom."
>
> Prophet Muhammad (pbuh) replies, "Oh Jabir…What dif-
> ficult conditions."

Benefits to the Community

The Month of Ramadan is known for the blessings that exist in the unity of community. Family and friends share a common experience for an entire month creating a bond that all look forward to year after year. There is a greater commitment to give charity to the needy and less fortunate. Often the month is filled with good deeds that outweigh the deeds for an entire year.

This charitable sense of stewardship gathers people in hundreds and even thousands to raise money for benevolent causes such as poverty and the plight of orphans around the world. That which is most rewarding and truly awesome is that the fasting person grows outside their immediate network and becomes part of a global unity. This feeling is intensified when one remembers that Muslims live in every country on earth, and fasting is happening throughout the world twenty-four hours a day as some people wake up to begin their fast, while others, on the other side of the world sit to break their fast.

This connection and collective remembrance of each other is a powerful unit in the fabric of Muslim life. The individual participates with humanity in praising, loving, sharing, and sacrificing for God. At the same time, each individual is the sole benefactor of God's mercy, kindness, and justice. God once again speaks to humankind through the revelation of the Holy Quran.

> When my servants ask thee concerning Me, I am indeed close to them: I listen to the prayer of every supplicant when he calleth upon Me: Let them, also with a will listen to My call and believe in Me: that they may walk in the right way.
>
> — *Quran, Chapter 2, The Cow, Al Baqarah, Verse 186*

Dos and Don'ts of Fasting

A fasting person refrains from things such as food, drink, smoke, and sexual intercourse from the time the sun rises until the sun sets at dusk. After the fast is broken, a person can resume normal activity. However, a person should continue to observe the most pious and excellent of all human conduct.

Fasting is a total undertaking and submission to developing a strong will and mind. A person must not gossip, lie, covet, steal, and bear false names against God or His Messengers including Adam, Noah, Abraham, Moses, Jesus, and Muhammad. This also includes such prominent members of the families of these Messengers like Eve, the Blessed Mother Mary, Khadija, the wife of Prophet Muhammad (pbuh) and their holy family. Others such as Harun (Aaron), Dawud (David), Suleiman (Solomon), Yusef (Joseph), Yeihyah, (John the Baptist), Yunus (Jonas), and Zachariah are among such prominent and religious figures in human history.

A person must not break family relations or ties. In fact, resuming family connections are very important during the month of fast.

During this month, everything multiplies and glorifies in the presence of the Omnipotent and Forgiving God. The mindset or mental preparation for the fast is as important as the fast itself. When the Prophet Muhammad (pbuh) took to his fast, he would recite this beautiful supplication to God:

> Oh God, be pleased with my fasts in this month as Thou gives credit to those who sincerely observe the fast. In addition, be pleased with my special night prayers in this month, as Thou gives credit to those who pray sincerely throughout the night. Direct me to be on guard and pay attention to free myself from the lethargy of forgetfulness. O the God of the worlds, overlook my wrong doings and grant amnesty to me. O He who shows sympathy and mercy to those who do wrong.
>
> — *Prophet Muhammad (pbuh)*

For Muslims and for non-Muslim readers especially, it is important to clarify a key point in Islam – that every Prophet and Messenger is granted a sinless nature and immunity from wrong doings by God. However, the Prophet Muhammad (pbuh) and the other Prophets and Messengers supplicated God in the most humble manner – as in this prayer above – to model for humanity how to call upon God the most Merciful in our own lives. As the Divinely Commanded Messengers showed us prayers like this, their teaching was for our sake, because these Messengers themselves could do no wrong, Islam teaches us.

Making Your Intention or Niyyah to Begin Your Fast

It is a fundamental belief in Islam that your deeds will be your scale on the Day of Judgment, which is the eternal tribunal of God. This day everything in creation will stand for their promise of Paradise or lack thereof. The Month of Ramadan is a most merciful month in which God promises forgiveness to those who pray and fast with sincerity of heart, mind, and spirit.

Niyyah is an Arabic word which means "intent" or "to have the intention of." Having Niyyah or intention is the intellectual exercise that has to precede the physical fast. In other words, it is the intellectual intentionality to begin the fast for the Holy Month. When a person begins with this intention to fast, it is with an even greater goal, which is to gain closeness to the Divine.

This closeness is an intellectual and spiritual ascent known as Qurba. This goal of Qurba or attaining a deeper and more profound closeness to the Divine — is the process of aligning with the commandments of God. Niyyah or intentionality need not be spoken by the tongue, but rather determined by the conscious mind to embark upon a specific act of worship. For the Month of Ramadan, it is sufficient for a person to decide that in obedience to God he or she will refrain from any act that may invalidate the fast from the time of the call for dawn prayer up to the time of the evening call to prayer.

Many people misunderstand the concept of Niyyah and believe that they must utter the intention verbally and aloud as in a proclamation and this is not true. There are two acceptable ways to make your intention. Every night a person can renew their intention to fast the following day, or a person may make their intention or Niyyah at the beginning of Ramadan, *one time*, with the intention of fasting the entire month. It is preferable to make your intention for the whole month since one may forget to renew the intention daily. It is also highly recommended but not mandatory to take a full ritual shower called a Ghusl or bath and then pray two units dedicated to your intention to fast.

In Islam, the intellect is golden, and God consciousness is the goal, therefore the first step for the fast is to internalize the intention be it spoken or silently in the heart. A simple example of a stated intention could be the following:

O God, Most Gracious, Most Merciful, I make my intention to fast the Holy Month of Ramadan seeking spiritual closeness and nearness to You. I ask that You accept my fast and deeds.

The Holy Prophet Muhammad (pbuh) had many beautiful supplications before worship. One such supplication demonstrates a very proactive form of worship:

"O Allah, (God), assist me in this Month of Ramadan to observe fast in its days and worship Thee in its nights. Restrain me from indulging in frivolities and transgressing the Divine Laws. Keep me alive praising Thee day in and day out through Thy guidance and Grace O the Guide of those who are apt to go astray."

— *Prophet Muhammad (pbuh)*

Who Is Exempt from the Fast?

There are a few groups of people who are exempt or excused from the fast. We will go through these groups briefly. Children under the age of physical maturation are exempt. By the age of 9 or 10, girls are often showing primary and secondary signs of physical maturation. Boys tend to show these primary and secondary signs of physical maturation around the age of 12 to 15. If these physical hallmarks are present then the fast should begin for either boys or girls. Menses and nocturnal emission are two sure signs of the physical readiness. Even if the adolescent or early teen is not physically mature but is mentally prepared, their fast can begin.

It is always amazing to see children as young as 6 and 7 begging to fast half the day, or skip either a breakfast or lunch to feel part of the excitement. We see other children taking on the intention of fasting as early as 9 and 10 years of age, though it is not mandatory for them yet. When the Month of Ramadan falls in the winter months, the fast is short and many children begin their fast at earlier ages.

The elderly are exempt when the fast becomes a hardship on their bodies. They are completely exempt with no need to make up their fast at a later time and no need to pay a charitable donation to compensate for the fast. The strong and able senior is still obligated to the fast so long as it does not impede health in any way. God does not wish hardship upon them. If they choose not to fast, then the charity tax to feed the hungry is the compensation. The charitable compensation should be equivalent to feeding one poor person for each day missed.

The sick are exempt but are required to make up their fasting days within the year prior to the following Ramadan. The pregnant and nursing mother is also exempt, for whom the fast brings potential harm to either her or the baby, with the intention to make the fast up before the following Ramadan. The same requirement for charitable compensation must be paid to the needy. The post-partum mother who is still experiencing the discharge of birth is exempt and falls under the rule of feeding the poor the equivalent of a day's food. The female experiencing her menses is also exempt from those days only and must make the fast up before the following Ramadan.

The traveling individual or person on a journey that must leave the metropolitan city limits and venture outside the boundary of their city (22 km or approximately 15 miles) is exempt and must make the day or days up within the year. This is not to suggest that if they live in a metro city such as Detroit, Chicago, New York and so on, they are limited to a 15-mile radius of their home. The rule is that a journey is defined by leaving the larger city limits and its usual suburbs. A divine loophole for those who must travel beyond the city limits is to leave after the noontime prayer has passed. This keeps the fast valid.

The Holy Quran lays out the many guidelines for the fast and what is not specific in the revelation is further defined by the Prophet Muhammad (pbuh). God once again speaks to humankind in the commandment of fast to help us understand the nature of the fast and the exemptions.

> O' those who have believed! Prescribed for you is a formal
> fast as it was for those before you, so that you would be
> God fearing. Fasting is prescribed for a fixed number of
> days. Then, whoever among you is sick or on a journey,
> (for them) a period of other days; and for those who can, a

redemption of food for the needy; and whoever volunteers good, it is better for him/her; but that the formal fast is best for you if you were to know. The month of Ramadan is one in which the Quran was sent forth as a guidance for humanity; with clear portents of the guidance, and the criterion between right and wrong; so whoever of you bears witness to the month, then he should formally fast it; and whoever is sick or on a journey, then a period of other days. God wants ease for you, and wants not hardship for you so that you complete the period and that you magnify God, because He guided you so that perhaps you would give thanks.

— *Quran, Chapter 2, Al Baqarah, The Cow, Verses 183 to 186*

Situations That Can Invalidate Your Fast

For Muslims there are conditions that change the nature of the fast. Both in Islamic history and in contemporary times, scholars debate the issues that govern the fast.

Obviously if someone is ill then God excuses the fast. However there are everyday encounters beyond illness that may change the nature of the fast. Many laws have to deal with precautionary measures that do not further dehydrate the body or risk anything reaching the back of the mouth and into the digestive system, such as smoking, or sitting in a hot whirlpool which can cause the body to sweat vigorously. Still other laws focus on moral alignment such as lying and swearing in the Name of God, and yet still other rules focus on physical pleasures such as the avoidance of sex during the fasting hours.

Consider the following digest of "don'ts" during Ramadan. Some of the following issues will be helpful especially to health-care professionals, counselors and chaplains as well as individuals and family members facing health concerns during the month. For non-Muslims reading this section, think about how reverently Muslims approach their faith and their commitment to the fast as they carefully consider these issues.

1. Ascribing False Names or Lies to God.

    a. If a person who is observing fast *intentionally* ascribes something false to God and His Prophets in writing or by a gesture or sign, then the fast becomes invalid even if he/she may at once retract the lie and repent for it.

2. Eating and Drinking

    a. If a fasting person *intentionally* eats or drinks even if it is a grain of rice or a drop of water then the fast becomes invalid. Make-up days need to be completed by the following Ramadan. Consult an imam or Muslim online resources in determining the requirements for charitable compensation and making up days of fasting, when situations like this arise.

    b. There is no harm in swallowing one's phlegm or mucous from the head and chest unless it comes up and reaches the mouth, then one should discharge it from the mouth and not swallow it.

    c. If a person *unintentionally* eats a bite of something or sips a liquid and quickly realizes what they did, the fast may continue. This may happen especially the first few days when the brain is still warming up to the idea that it may not eat.

3. Sexual Coitus (Intercourse) During Fasting Hours

    a. Sexual intercourse between spouses invalidates the fast, even if penetration is minimal.

4. Masturbation or Istimna.

    a. If a person, observing fast participates in masturbation then their fast become invalid.

b. If a fasting person falls asleep, as in a nap, and a nocturnal emission/or wet dream causes orgasm and discharge of bodily fluid, the fast is not invalidated. However, the person is now in a state of ritual impurity known as *Janaba* and requires a ritual shower called *Ghusl* to return to the state of purity. The shower should not be delayed. As with all things in Islam, the ritual shower begins with the intentionality to wash from the impurities of the body to gain closeness *(Qurba)* to God. The head is first washed along with the neck and preferably the right side of the body then the left, however most importantly the head first and body second.

5. The Ritual Shower after Sexual Intercourse, Menses, and Post Partum Bleeding.

a. If a person in *Janaba* (condition after sexual union) does not take *Ghusl* (the ritual shower) intentionally until the time of dawn prayers, his/her fast becomes invalid. The fast must begin in the state of ritual purity to be valid.

b. If a person is in *Janaba* during the night and knows that if he/she goes to sleep with the risk of not waking up to shower before the dawn prayer, then the shower must be taken before sleep to avoid such a risk. If he/she sleeps until dawn prayers therefore missing the opportunity to shower, the fast will be void, and must be made up with an obligation for repentance for that missed day of fast. This rule also requires further research by the fasting person. The repentance compensation stems from an alert and conscious decision to delay the act of ritual purity and has specific rules about how to make up the day of fast.

c. If a woman gets her natural menstrual cycle anytime during the observance of fast she must consider the day invalid and repeat it before the next Ramadan. There are many rules that apply to female reproduction and menses. It is advisable to seek counsel or consult books on Islamic law, concerning these issues if you are uncertain about the answers. One such resource is by one of the most learned scholars in the Muslim world today. The Grand Ayatollah Sayed Ali Al-Husaini Sistani's book on Islamic Law outlines the conditions and rules for many of the concerns often raised by women concerning their natural cycles, post partum and post menses questions. Information regarding Islamic law can be found at Islamic Libraries online as well. In addition, most scholars of jurisprudence have online offices that receive questions that pertain to daily life with a fair-to-adequate response time. If an urgent answer is needed, it is best to contact your local scholar or a learned person to help guide you.

d. If a female becomes clear of her cycle or post-baby bleeding just near the time of dawn prayer in the month of Ramadan, and has no time left for the ritual shower or *Ghusl* her fast is valid and she should proceed with her shower. One must recognize Islam's care and intimate connection with the human condition. Most every scenario and situation has a different law that rules or governs the condition. The rules for female menses may be different from the rules for sexual union and so on. It is God's mercy and love for humanity that has given us this blueprint so that the closeness or *Qurba*, is realized in a prescribed way.

e. The usual rule is that a menstrual cycle is not less than three days or more than ten days. If it is less than three days or more than ten days the rules change to a condition known as *Istihadha*, which is also a blood-like discharge but not considered to be the monthly cycle. A female who experiences bleeding other than the normal menstrual cycle is in a state of *Istihadha* for whom fasting is obligatory. This is often the case for women who have intermittent discharge usually associated with menopause. Again, these rules are online and in various other published resources if you need further guidance.

6. Ingesting thick smoke and dust — and smoking.

   a. Based on obligatory precaution, allowing thick dust to reach one's throat invalidates the fast. This is true whether the dust is of something that is allowable *(halal)* to eat like flour or of something that is not allowable *(haraam)* to consume like dust or earth. Cigarette smoke such as second-hand smoke should be avoided as well. Smoking in general invalidates the fast. Recently, there has been some examination of this rule, but the majority of Muslim intellects and scholars agree that smoking invalidates the fast even if the smoke does not reach the throat.

7. Immersing the head in water.

   a. It is not recommended and by some scholars forbidden to immerse the entire head in water while fasting. According to the Grand Ayatollah Sistani's rule on this issue, immersing the head in water does not invalidate your fast, but it is not recommended.

   b. This rule does not apply to showering but rather would apply to something like underwater swimming. For students in school this could be problematic if swimming is part of their physical education requirements. A letter from your local Muslim center will help to excuse underwater swimming.

8. Enemas

   a. If a fasting person takes a liquid enema, his/her fast becomes invalid even if he is obliged to take it for the sake of treatment.

9. Vomiting

a. *Intentional* vomiting invalidates the fast. (However, remember that the fast should be broken if a person is ill.) The fast does not become invalid if someone vomits involuntarily perhaps from a nauseating sight, smell, or taste.

Strongly discouraged behaviors for a fasting person.

- Using eye drops.

- Applying eyeliner (*kohl*) if its taste or smell reaches the throat.

- Performing an act that causes general weakness like blood-letting or giving blood.

- Hot baths such as whirlpools or saunas that can increase dehydration.

- Inhaling things such as tobacco or snuff that can reach the throat.

- Smelling fragrant herbs and fruits, which may stimulate hunger.

- Using suppositories inserted in the rectum as bowel stimulants, which may lead to dehydration.

- Remaining in clothing that becomes wet, which may cause shivering and perhaps result in loss of energy reserve.

- Getting a tooth extracted or doing something that may cause bleeding of the mouth.

Precaution should be used to keep the body as healthy as possible during the fast. Use reasonable parameters. Many student and professional athletes manage to fast and play aggressive sports. That may be a reasonable choice for them, because their bodies are in top condition.

Many pregnant and lactating women maintain their fast especially during the winter months without any consequences such as dehydration. The University of Michigan in a qualitative research study by Trinka Robbins, a Nurse Midwife, reports pregnant women fasting without ill effects. However, it is critical to be reasonable during the fast. Getting plenty of rest, frequent naps, good and healthy foods high in protein and fiber at breakfast *(Sahoor)* and at dinner *(Iftar)* help to maintain a normal healthy status. Drinking a lot of water before and after the fast while limiting caffeinated beverages is encouraged.

The lists I have shared above are not exhaustive. They are intended to outline common questions experienced by men and women who are fasting as well as health-care providers, chaplains and family members caring for people with challenging physical conditions.

Logic and reason should prevail in following these rules.

Behaviors That Do NOT Invalidate Your Fast

As before, consider the following list as common examples of behaviors that people may question during Ramadan – but that do *not* invalidate the fast. Once again, some of these issues will be helpful to health-care professionals, counselors and chaplains as well as individuals and family members. If you are caring for Muslim patients during Ramadan, there are many easy and reasonable adjustments you can make to accommodate these sacred traditions. For example, adjust meal times so that breakfast is served before dawn and the evening meal comes after dusk.

Here are examples of common issues that arise – but these do ***not*** invalidate the fast.

- Nose bleeds.

- Giving blood without causing general weakness.

- Receiving blood.

- IV fluids.

- Eye, ear and nose drops (nose drops should not be swallowed through the throat)

- Inhalers for asthma or respiratory conditions so long as the mist reaches the lungs.

- Tooth extractions or cleanings as long as blood or water is not swallowed.

- Brushing one's teeth without swallowing water.

- Injections like heparin, insulin, vaccinations and antibiotics.

- Removing clothing for medical treatments like X-Rays.

- Chewing food to feed a child.

- Tasting the food while cooking for those who will break their fast in your home does not invalidate the fast even if it happens to reach the throat inadvertently.

- Unintentionally swallowing food or drink due to forgetfulness.

- The examination of genitals such as deemed medically necessary for men or women does not invalidate your fast. Rectal exams, breast exams or vaginal exams may take place during Ramadan.

Making Up Your Fast and Paying Charity

In the following situations, both compensations – making up days of fasting and contributions to charity — are obligatory. There are different forms of charitable compensation *(Kaffarah)* and various other rules involved here, but this section is intended as a general guideline to illustrate how these issues work in Islam. These compensations become obligatory when the following acts are committed *intentionally*, which means voluntarily and without any force or pressure, during the fast.

1. Eating

2. Drinking

3. Sexual Intercourse

4. Sexual Self Stimulation / Masturbation

5. Staying in the state of ritual impurity until the time of dawn prayers

6. Ascribing False Names or Lies to God

7. Ingesting smoke and dust

8. Full body immersion under water

9. Enemas

10. Intentional vomiting

Kaffarah for These Intentional Acts

Islam spells out penalties for men and women compensating for these failings. Among them are:

1. To give freedom to a slave. Although most people no longer have contact with the slavery that still exists in some parts of our modern world, this is a traditional example of *Kaffarah* listed in Islam. Even though freeing a slave today would be very difficult for most people, its inclusion in this common list illustrates Islam's commitment to abolishing this oppressive human condition.

2. Fast two consecutive months for every day intentionally missed without an excuse such as travel or illness. This is a very steep penalty and further reinforces Islam's emphasis on the accountability of the intellect, which has a free will to choose its destiny.

3. Feeding 60 people to their fill or giving one *mudd*, pronounced "mood", an Arabic measurement equivalent to approximately 750 grams of food. This can take the form of staples such as dates, rice, barely, wheat, bread and raisins to each of the 60 people. The food proportion should be based on what a person's meal would be for the day. *Muud* is an approximation of what the human stomach needs to sustain the human body.

Islam is a practical faith. If it is not possible for a person to fulfill any of the above rules (perhaps due to a person's limited income), then a charitable compensation *(Sadaqa)* is paid in accordance with the person's means. Also seeking forgiveness and repentance from God is necessary. The nature of the repentance should be to avoid the same intentional act that broke the fast in the first place.

As an obligatory precaution, the person also should intend to pay the charitable penalty as soon as he/she is capable of doing so. Remember that a *Kaffarah* is paid as a penitence for a sin, while a *Sadaqa* is supposed to be paid as a good deed. Muslims pay *Sadaqa* or charity throughout the year while *Kaffarah* is paid to reduce or erase a sin that one truly regrets making.

When considering these issues I have outlined in these pages, it is important to remember that there clearly are many other acts – some of them far more serious than the actions listed above – that invalidate the fast. Obviously, some people commit very serious sins. Reconciling yourself as a Muslim after some actions can be a complex process and Muslims often turn to imams, counselors and other religious scholars to help resolve such issues. What I have written here is not intended to be exhaustive of all troubling behaviors. It's simply a helpful guide to many common issues faced by Muslims, professional caregivers, family and friends during Ramadan.

A Few Other Situations That Commonly Arise

A woman must make up the days she missed due to her monthly cycle before the next Ramadan but does not have to pay a retribution charity.

If a person does not fast in the month of Ramadan due to illness and the illness continues until next Ramadan, it is not obligatory to observe the previous fast. For each fast, he should give one portion of food (one *mudd*) like wheat, barley, bread, etc. to the poor.

If a person does not observe the fast due to traveling or some other excuse, he/she should perform the make-up fast and also as an obligatory precaution give one portion of food to the poor. There are many rules that apply to the person who travels as a means of living – another example of complex issues that should involve advice from a scholar.

Night of Destiny, Fate, Power

During this month by the graciousness and mercy of God, the merits of your deeds are multiplied. The Prophet Muhammad (pbuh) shares with us that evil spirits such as Satan and Satan's associates are imprisoned this month. This is to imply that we have more immunity against the evil lurkings of Satan. Muslims really feel the abundant blessings of this month. The month is certainly filled with a different feeling of reverence for God and a deepening spiritual awareness. The Prophet Muhammad (pbuh) urged us to approach this month in this way.

> Whosoever performs a recommended prayer this month,
> God will keep the fire of hell away from you. Your prayers
> are worship and whosoever performs an obligatory prayer,
> God will reward him with seventy prayers in this month.
> He who recites one verse of Holy Quran will be given the
> reward of reciting the entire Quran during other months.
>
> — *Prophet Muhammad (pbuh)*

The Night of Destiny, Fate and Power: Laylat al-Qadr

A major component of the Holy Month of Ramadan is the incredible Night of Divine Power, as many refer to this special observance. This is a night of Spiritual Grandeur like no other night throughout the year. It has been said, perhaps in symbolic terms, that this night literally sets the determination for mercy until the following month of Ramadan.

The specific night is not clearly known but indications are that it happens on an odd night during the last ten days of the Holy Month of Ramadan. The Prophet Muhammad (pbuh) and his family have indicated that the 19th, 21st, and 23rd days of Ramadan are critical opportunities for spiritual advancement. Some very prominent scholars and intellects of Islam conclude from the teachings of the Holy Prophet and his family that the 23rd is most likely the Night of Power and Grandeur. No day or night throughout the year is comparable to the incomprehensible magnificence of this night.

The Holy Quran tells us that the night of Qadr is greater than one thousand months. Contemplate and comprehend the glory and majesty of God, and His mercy upon humankind this night. Think about how much God must love and favor humanity for bestowing upon the universe and creation this awesome night. In this night the Great Spirit, thought to be the Arch Angel Gabriel along with thousands of Angels descend upon earth by God's command. The earth will be filled with Angels that hear our prayers and by God's decree bring the destiny and fate of humankind to the awaited savior and messiah. Our supplications and prayers are heard and granted when good for us. This night should be regarded as the mark of our new year setting the stage for the year to come.

One of the Divine Wisdoms or Hadith Al Qudsi says that Angel Gabriel will descend upon earth bringing greetings of peace, (salaam) to every faithful Muslim except for the Muslim that consumes swine and alcohol. This is *not* a night in which God will grant us things that may cause us more harm than good. God hears the humble cries for mercy and provides enlightenment that could free our souls and help us attain nearness to Him. This night helps to illuminate the heart and soul of the faithful believer. Keep in mind that the days are also auspicious so one should recite the Holy Quran and supplicate or dialogue with the Creator. God has given this night its special place in the Holy Quran by describing it in His own words. In the Arabic language of the Holy Quran, there is only one way to say each heavenly word, however in English and other languages we must rely on translation to grasp the deep meaning of the Holy Quran, which often fails us in translation. Here we offer two translations that come fairly close to the Arabic words of revelation.

In the Name of God,

The Merciful, The Compassionate.

Truly — We sent it forth on the night of power.

What shall cause you to recognize

What is the night of power?

The night of power is better than a thousand months.

The Angels come forth, and the Spirit during it

With their Lord's permission, with every command.

Peace! It is until the time of the rising dawn.

— *Quran, Chapter 97, The Night of Power, Translated by Laleh Bakhtiar*

In the Name of God,

The Merciful, The Compassionate.

We have indeed revealed this (Message).

In the Night of Power.

And what will explain to thee what the Night of Power is?

The Night of Power is better than a thousand months.

Therein come down the angels and the Spirit (Gabriel)

By God's permission on every errand.

Peace! This until the rise of the Morn!

— Quran, Chapter 97, The Night of Power, Translated by Yusuf Ali

It is preferable and highly recommended to have a bath or shower just before sunset on these holy days. It is important to remember that any of these nights begins at sunset the day before. If you are preparing yourself for worship throughout the night of the 21st. then you shower and make your intention the evening of the 20th. As soon as the sun sets, your prayers and supplications should begin. If the sun sets at 8 p.m. on the 20th day of Ramadan, then you consider that the beginning of the 21st day.

To bring more clarity to this issue, since it seems to confuse many people, the last ten odd days begin with the 19th day of Ramadan and end with the 29th. Millions of Muslims spend these holy nights in spiritual vigils asking, begging and pleading God's Almighty Mercy.

Begin your prayers this way:

- Recite two units of prayers *(Sallat)*.

- After the recitation of the Opening Chapter *(Al' Fatiha)*, recite Chapter 112, The Sincere Expression *(Al Ikhlass)*, 7 times.

- After you are finished, repeat the following 70 times:

- I ask You God, for your forgiveness and I return repentant unto You.

The Prophet Muhammad (pbuh) offered the following advice about the Night of Power:

> Once someone asked the Holy Prophet (pbuh) what to ask God for on the Night of Power. The Holy Prophet (pbuh) advised him to beseech God for his deliverance on the Day of Judgment, saying:
>
> The person who has turned away from the mercy of God, has indeed forgone his opportunity to embrace the forgiveness of God.
>
> — *Prophet Muhammad (pbuh)*

When should the Night be observed? Viewpoints vary among the world's 1 billion Muslims on which night is proper for the observance. Millions believe that the 23rd day is rated above the 19th and 21st and a great number of Muslim traditions hold that the 23rd is the proper Laylat al-Qadr. However, it also is true that the dates of this observance vary within Islam. Many observe it on the 25th or 27th of the month. Consult your imam or Muslim centers in your area about this observance.

It is strongly urged that in order to maximize the benefits of this night the faithful should recite the following chapters of the Holy Quran between sunset and dawn of the following day:

- Spider *(Ankaboot)*, once

- Smoke *(Dukhaan)*, once

- Romans *(Room)*, once

- Night of Power *(Qadr)*, 1,000 times (or as many times as possible)

Reflection During the Night of Power

The night should then continue in deep spiritual soul searching beseeching the Almighty and Sublime God to guide us along the Straight Path. A humble servant would want to consider the plight of the world on these nights. Pray for the global good of the world, and the local good of our communities. End the night in personal prayers that will bring us closeness to God. Think about our position in life. Who are we, what are we, and why are we. Contemplate what special gift God has given to you so that you may fulfill your role in this life and contribute with your special gift to the betterment of humanity. Ask God to protect your family and health, and to continue to give you the sustenance that you need to live a dignified life.

Ask God to help strengthen your will to be a better Muslim, hence a better human being. Ask God to give us the wisdom to meet the challenges of our faith tenets. Ask God to keep your whole mind and body from great sins such as alcohol and swine, gambling and other such vices. Focus your self and pray long prostrations with your head to the ground where you create a cove of peace with your hands along side your head. Let that quiet time and position take you over into a new spiritual realm and ground you in a sense of peace and tranquility. God has said over and again to His creation many beautiful things, which are astounding when we reflect on them. We must all remember that the Holy Quran is God's conversation with humankind. When we wish to hear God, we should go to His book, when we wish for God to listen to us, we should cultivate and activate our sublime state of spiritual consciousness. On these nights, we should move our souls in a forward journey, taking at the very least steps toward renewal and ultimately a more intimate connection with the Divine Presence. Below are listed just three of many beautiful selections from the Holy Quran.

The first verse speaks about remembrance of God. This state of God-remembrance throughout the day can cultivate a deep tranquility and state of peace in our hearts and for our place in the world. The second verse is a beautiful conversation between the Creator and the created in which God invites His servant to invite Him into our hearts. He establishes an almost Divine Unique friendship with all who call upon

Him. This verse truly captures a state of humbleness and true humility in that God acknowledges His own presence in our daily lives by telling us that He listens to our prayers and invites us to listen and believe in Him. The third verse establishes a covenant between God and His servant. In this verse, God invites the soul that has reached the state of peace, or salaam, to return to its origin, and Lord God. To return to being pleased with what God has given us, and for us, in return, to be pleasing to our Lord. This is a unique love between the created and the Creator. In essence, this sums up our life mission on earth and the culmination of our belief and practices by the invitation to enter the heavenly and eternal abode.

> Those who believe and whose hearts find satisfaction (tranquility) in the remembrance of God; for without doubt in the remembrance of God, do hearts find satisfaction and tranquility.
>
> — *Quran, Chapter 13, The Thunder, Al Raad, Verse 28*

> When my servants ask thee concerning Me I am indeed close to them; I listen to the prayer of every servant when he calls upon Me; let them also, with a will, listen to My call and believe in Me; that they may walk in the right path.
>
> — *Quran, Chapter 2, The Cow, Al Baqarah, Verse 186*

> (To the righteous soul will be said;)
>
> O thou soul in complete rest and satisfaction!
>
> "Come back to thy Lord well pleased (you) and well – pleasing unto Him!
>
> "Enter thou among my Devotees! " And (invited are you) to enter my heaven!"
>
> — *Quran, Chapter 89, The Dawn, Al Fajr, Verses 27 - 30*

The End of Ramadan

The New Moon

Note that many Muslims may celebrate the end of the month on the 29th day depending on the sighting of the new moon and the position of the moon in the horizon. There are often debates each year on what is the actual day of the Holy Holiday — Eid. If you are new to Islam or on the outside looking in with Muslim co-workers or with Muslim friends, you may see a lot of confusion over the correct date of the Eid. You may find it strange that the Muslim world is not in agreement with the simple use of science and astronomy to indicate the birth of the new moon. Even within congregations and communities there could be variations and opinions. It would be wonderful for the worldwide Muslim community to celebrate on the same day. On the other hand, this diversity of approach to the birth of the new moon leaves room to have intellectually stimulating conversation and discourse over the verses in the Holy Quran. Did God mean that the new moon must be sighted by the human eye? Does a telescope equal the human eye? If science can predict the lunar calendar for years on end, is that not the advancement of the intellect which God loves so much and encourages? These debates have allowed for multiple holiday prayers within a congregation and communities that can expand the festivities to more than a day.

The Day of Eid

Remember: one must not fast on the day of eid.

It is highly desirable and recommended to read and recite as much of the Holy Quran as possible attempting to complete it entirely during the Month of Ramadan. The night before Eid is very precious and is regarded by God to be a glorious and very blessed night. Spend the night before Eid in long prostrations, invoking the name of God. The day of Eid is a celebration of the divine test that each fasting person has passed, with God's permission and will *(Insha'Allah)*. Eid is a day in which we celebrate our forgiveness gained through God's mercy.

Eid: Recommended But Not Mandatory Practices

On the morning of Eid, it is highly recommended to shower or bathe. Before bathing, it is highly desirable to say the following supplication:

O God, I am believing in Thee, Fully Aware of Thy Book, Following the way of life of Thy Prophet Muhammad (pbuh), peace and blessings be upon him and on his holy family.

Make your intention to take your bath or shower and afterward recite the following recommended supplication:

O God, let me make amends and compensate for my wrong doings, (so that) my religion becomes pure. In addition, I ask You to remove all impurities from me.

Eid: Giving of Charity and Alms

Give your obligatory prescribed charity *(Fitra)* on the day of Eid. If you are not sure how much you should pay then consult your religious leader or local mosque to see if there is a set amount. The amount is the equivalent of 3 kg. of wheat, barley, rice, dates, or raisins which amounts to approximately $7.00 to $10.00 per person in your household for the year. The Fitra must be set aside. It becomes obligatory on the eve before the Eid. However, if a person is unable to give prior to Eid prayer, he/she is still obligated to pay after the prayers on the same day or sometime later. The Fitra should be given to the local poor or needy relatives, exempting your parents and your children because these individuals are obligatory upon you in terms of financial needs. The head of the household should pay additional Fitra on behalf of all those persons who are breaking their fast or residing in their home the nightfall before Eid whether they be young or old, Muslims or not, irrespective of whether or not it is obligatory on him/ her to maintain them, and whether they live in his/ her own town, are visitors or reside outside of town.

To simplify this important rule, anyone who is in your home the night before Eid becomes apart of your Fitra charity and you must pay on their behalf unless they have paid their own Fitra and excuse you of the responsibility. *(Rule 2001 Islamic Laws –Seestani)*

Eid: Clothing and Other Traditions

Islam places a great emphasis on cleanliness, personal hygiene, and appearance. On the day of Eid, it is tradition to purchase new and clean clothing if you are financially able. It is highly advisable for Muslim men to practice the manner of applying cologne or fragrance, as did the Holy Prophet (pbuh). The Prophet Muhammad (pbuh) was known to have a beautiful clean and appealing presence in his personal and community life. Before going for Eid prayers, it is also advisable to eat breakfast, dates or any other sweet dish perhaps to equalize the blood sugar levels and give the celebrating Muslim strength for the day. It is highly advisable to pray the Eid prayers in congregation; also, to gather afterward as family and friends, and pay respect to parents and the elders. It is also recommended to visit the ill and also the graves of loved ones. Islam believes the soul never dies and can hear the visitors of the graves. Toys, gifts of money, and other such specialties are often shared with children, which make the day of Eid a special memory.

Beautiful Praises of God

Praises of the Divine *(Takbeerat)* for Eid are highly recommended and should be recited beginning the night before the holiday, at the end of the evening prayers and also on the morning of Eid after dawn prayers.

> God is Greatest, God is Greatest, There is no God Save
> God, and God is Greatest, God is Greatest. All praise is
> to God. We sing the praises of God because He has shown
> us the straight path. We gratefully thank Him because He
> takes care of us and looks after our interests.

Eid Mubarak, Insha'Allah (With God's Will)
Ramadhan 2008.

Appendix

A Supplication for this month: Duaa Al Iftitah

This is a prayer shared by millions of Muslims around the world during the Holy Month of Ramadan. Many Muslims try to read this supplication daily throughout the month-long fast. The English wording may vary slightly from one version to another. Some use "Allah," an Arabic word for "God." Here is the text:

O God, I begin the glorification with praise of Thee; Thou, from Thy bounties, gives out freely the truth and salvation; I know for certain that Thou art the most merciful in disposition of forgiveness and mercy, [but] very exacting at the time of giving exemplary punishment and chastisement to wrongdoers, the Omnipotent in the domain of absolute power and might.

O God, Thou has given me permission to invoke Thee and beseech Thee, so listen, O Hearer, to my words of praise, and give a favorable reply to my supplication, and minimize my falling into misery, O the often-forgiving. O my God, many a trouble Thou hath removed; many a sorrow hath Thou dispelled; many a misery hath Thou mitigated; and at all times Thou spreadeth out mercy, and cutteth short the tightening circles of misfortunes. All praise is to God, Who has not taken unto Himself a wife, or a son, and Who has no partner in sovereignty, nor any protecting friend through dependence. Magnify Him with all magnificence.

All praise is to God, with full gratitude for all his bounties. All praise is to God, Who has no opposition to His rule, nor any challenge to His commands.

All praise belongs to God, Who has no counsel to meddle with His operation of creation, nor is there anything similar to Him in His greatness. All praise is to God, Whose commandments operate in Creation; His glory is evident through love and kindness. His distinct overflowing generosity is freely available through His unlimited bestowals, which do not exhaust His resources, and He does not swell the numerous benefits except because of generosity and kindness. Verily He is mighty, generous.

O Lord, I ask for some from much, in the midst of my very many needs for which I entirely depend on Thee, and, since eternity, Thou art able to do without it but for me it is a titanic effort and for Thee is very easy and simple. O God, truly, when Thou pardon my sins, overlook my mistakes, take a lenient view of my disorderly conduct, cover up my foul actions, show consideration in spite of my many transgressions committed willfully or negligently, I am tempted to ask for that which I do not deserve, from Thee Who, through Thy mercy, gives me the daily bread, provides me with that which is suitable for me, through Thy control; and distinguishes me with a favorable reply to my requests. So I persist in calling out, believing in Thee, and I invoke Thee, talking familiarly, not afraid, nor shy, but assured of Thy love and kindness whenever I turn to Thee. A temporary setback and I, out of ignorance, begin to despair, although perhaps slowing down may be a blessing in disguise, because Thou alone knows [all] the consequences.

I know no generous Master who is more accommodating to unsatisfied servants as Thou art to me.

O Lord, Thou giveth an invitation but I turn it down. Thou becometh familiar with me but I do not care for Thee. Thou loveth me but I do not correspond to Thee as if Thou are overreaching me. Yet Thou doth not abstain from bestowing favors and blessings on me from Thy mercy and generosity so have mercy on Thy ignorant servant Verily Thou art generous and kind. Praise is To God the owner of sovereignty, Who sets the course of the skies and the stars controls the winds, causes the daybreak, and administers authority, the Lord of the worlds. Praise is to God for His indulgence in the wake of His all-awareness. Praise is to God for His amnesty ensuing from His omnipotence. Praise is To God for the respite He allows In spite of provocation. He is able to do what He wills. Praise be to God, the Creator of all the created beings, Who makes sustenance freely available, starts the day, the owner of glory, might, favors, and bounties, Who is far away, invisible, and nearest, so near that He is fully aware of the whispered secrets, the Blessed, the Praised.

Praise is to God, Who has no equal to challenge Him, nor is there an image comparable to Him, nor a helper to assist Him. He tames the powerful by His force, and disgraced are the terrible before His greatness, so He, through His power, fulfils that which He wills. Praise is to God, Who gives answer to me whenever I call Him; covers up my shortcomings yet I disobey Him; gives me the largest part of the bounties yet I want more. Many favors He has sanctioned; many terrible dangers He has averted; and many blossoming joys he has made available for me. Therefore, I sing His praises and recite His glorifications. Praise is to God. None can disclose anything hidden by Him; none can shut the doors kept open by Him; no one who makes a request is sent away disappointed by Him; and no one who looks long and attentively is deluded in his hopes.

Praise be to God, Who gives protection to the frightened; comes to the help of the upright; promotes the cause of the weak and the enslaved; annihilates the autocrats; destroys rulers and appoints the 'awaited saviors' in their place. Praise be to God, Who breaks everything belonging to the oppressors; puts an end to the tyrants; watches over the fugitives; brings assistance to those who cry out for help; meets and clears up the demands of the needy beseechers; supports the faithful.

Praise be to God, In his awe-inspiring fear the heavens and its dwellers tremble and shiver; the earth and its inhabitants shake and quiver; the oceans and all that floats and swims in its waters flow together in excitement and tumult. Praise is to God, Who has guided us to this. We could not truly have been led aright if God had not guided us. Praise be to God, Who creates but is not created; gives subsistence but needs no provisions; gives food to eat but takes no nourishment; makes the living dead and brings the dead to life; and He is the ever living, there is no death for Him; in His hands is all the good. Moreover, He is able to do all things.

O God, send blessings on Muhammad, Thy servant, Messenger, confidant, friend, beloved intimate, mercy unto all the created beings, bearer of Thy sacraments, quotient of Thy messengers, the most superior, the exquisite, the most handsome, the most perfect, the upright, the more prospering, the more pleasant, the thoroughly purified, the sublime; who has more and better blessings, advantages, mercies, affections and salutations than Thou made available to any one of Thy servants, friends, and those honored by Thee from among Thy created being.

Send Your Blessings O Lord Upon All Of Your Messengers and Prophets Throughout Our Human History with a

Special Blessing Upon Noah, Abraham, Moses, Jesus and Muhammad and their Holy Families.

References

For Further Reading

The following titles were among the books consulted in preparing this guide. They are good choices for further reading.

Islamic Laws, Ayatullah al Uzaman Syed Ali al Husaini Seestani, The World Federation, Stanmore Middx U.K.

Supplication Prayers and Ziarats, Call on Me I answer You. Ansariyan Publications, Qum, Iran.

The Holy Quran, Abdulah Yusuf Ali, Thrike Tarsile Quran, Inc. New York, Kazi Publications, Chicago, IL.

The Sublime Quran, Laleh Bakhtiar, Kazi Publications, Chicago, Ill

www.ingramcontent.com/pod-product-compliance
Lightning Source LLC
Chambersburg PA
CBHW060428090426
42734CB00011B/2492